GEOMETRIC PATTERNS
AND HOW TO CREATE THEM

CLARENCE P. HORNUNG

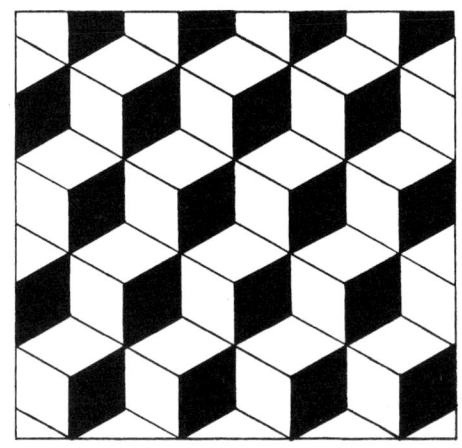

DOVER PUBLICATIONS, INC.
Mineola, New York

Copyright

Copyright © 2001 by Dover Publications, Inc.
All rights reserved under Pan American and International Copyright Conventions.

Published in Canada by General Publishing Company, Ltd., 30 Lesmill Road, Don Mills, Toronto, Ontario.

Bibliographical Note

Geometric Patterns and How to Create Them is a new work, first published by Dover Publications, Inc., in 2001.

DOVER *Pictorial Archive* SERIES

This book belongs to the Dover Pictorial Archive Series. You may use the designs and illustrations for graphics and crafts applications, free and without special permission, provided that you include no more than ten in the same publication or project. (For permission for additional use, please write to Permissions Department, Dover Publications, Inc., 31 East 2nd Street, Mineola, N.Y. 11501.)

However, republication or reproduction of any illustration by any other graphic service, whether it be in a book or in any other design resource, is strictly prohibited.

International Standard Book Number: 0-486-41733-6

Manufactured in the United States of America
Dover Publications, Inc., 31 East 2nd Street, Mineola, N.Y. 11501

CONTENTS

Equilateral Triangles, figures 1–8 2
Isosceles Triangles, figures 9–16 4
Right-Angle Triangles, figures 17–24 6
Triangles and Diamonds, figures 25–28 8
Obtuse Triangles, figures 29–32 9
Squares, figures 33–40 10
Tilted Squares, figures 41–48 12
Alternating Rectangles, figures 49–52 14
Horizontal Rectangles, figures 53–56 15
Tilted Rectangles, figures 57–64 16
Paired Rectangles, figures 65–68 18
Rectangular Basketweave, figures 69–72 19
Diamonds, figures 73–80 20
Alternating Diamonds, figures 81–88 22
Horizontal Diamonds, figures 89–96 24
Vertical Diamonds, figures 97–104 26
Diamonds and Cubes, figures 105–120 28
Diamonds and Tilted Squares, figures 121–128 32
Diamonds and Bisected Squares, figures 129–132 34
Arrangement of Diamonds, figures 133–136 35
Arrangement of Hexagons, figures 137–152 36
Arrangement of Octagons, figures 153–160 40
Arrangement of Squares, figures 161–164 42

INTRODUCTION

In this idea-rich sampler of geometric patterns based on several basic shapes, renowned designer Clarence Hornung has provided the means for anyone who can produce straight lines to invent an almost endless array of dazzling designs. For each group of designs—developed from one basic shape or a combination of two—a pattern grid is provided. This is followed by various sample designs, created by making alternate shapes in the grid black, in diverse patterns. Many of the patterns produce optical illusions, as the contrasting areas of black and white give the impression of three-dimensionality and sometimes even seem to be separated by curved lines. Most of the images formed can be perceived in at least two different ways by people viewing them. By using this method, an almost infinite number of designs can be developed. The addition of color adds still another dimension to the patterns.

Besides being a magnificent resource for incipient designers, *Geometric Patterns and How to Create Them* is a versatile source of copyright-free designs that can be used as bands, borders, or all-over patterns in many art and crafts projects, including needlework such as bargello, crochet, and quilting. Anyone, amateur or professional, beginner or expert, can enjoy creatively exploring the myriad patterns that can be invented by both repeated and varied arrangements of the selected geometric shapes.

GEOMETRIC PATTERNS
AND HOW TO CREATE THEM

Equilateral Triangles

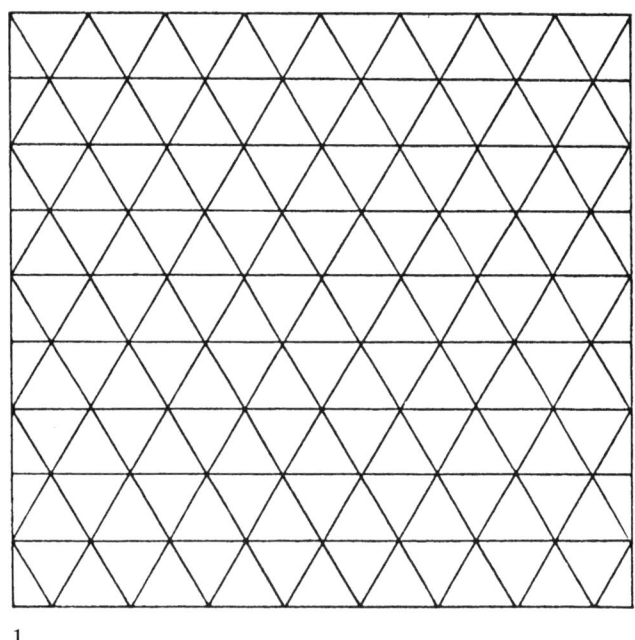

1

2

3

4

Equilateral Triangles

5

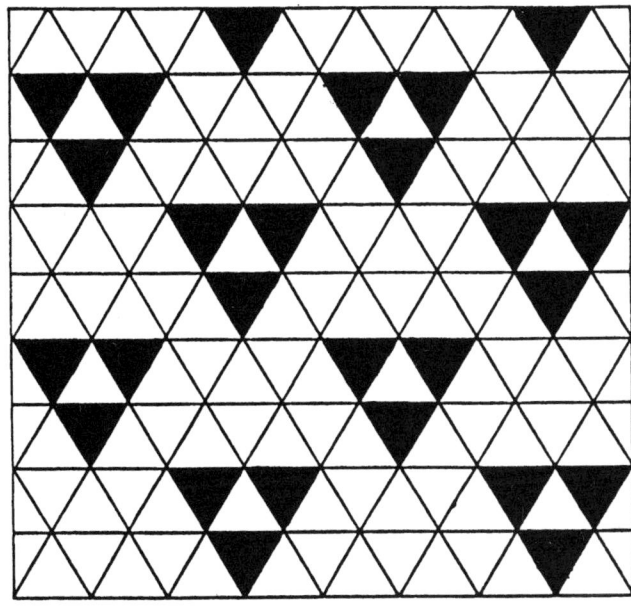

6

7

8

Isosceles Triangles

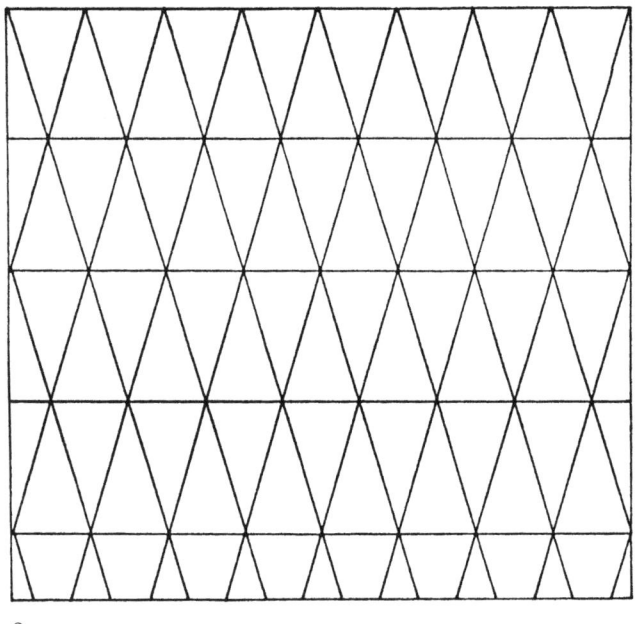

9

10

11

12

Isosceles Triangles

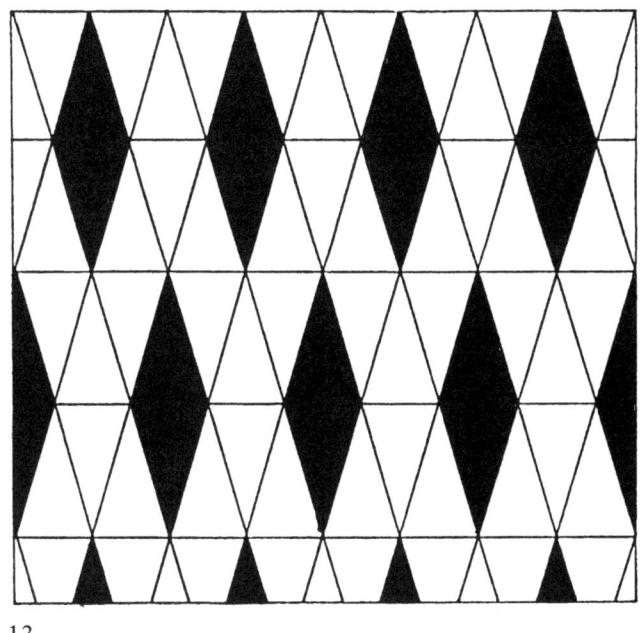
13

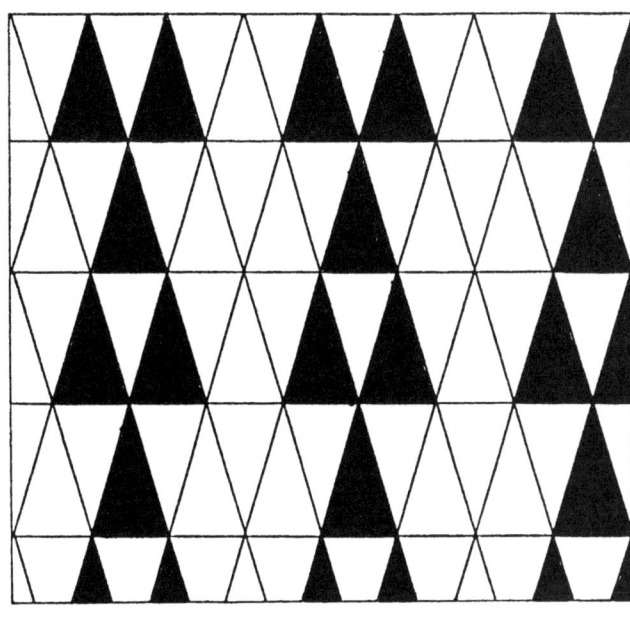
14

15

16

Right-Angle Triangles

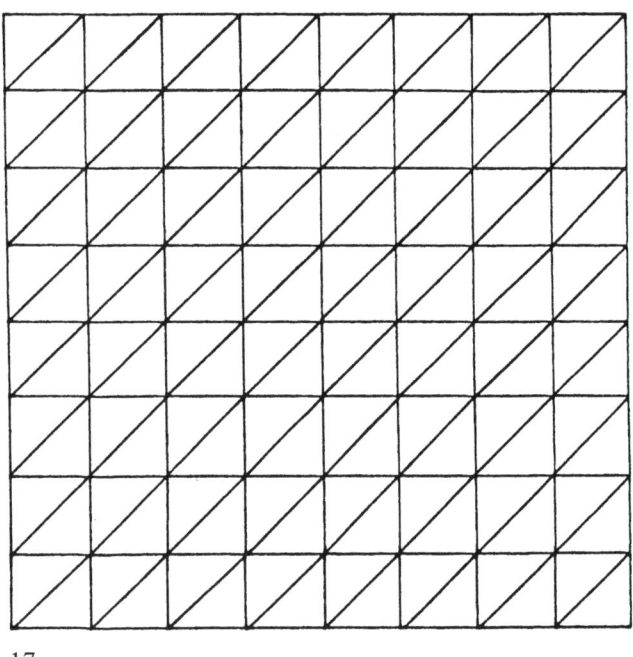

17

18

19

20

Right-Angle Triangles

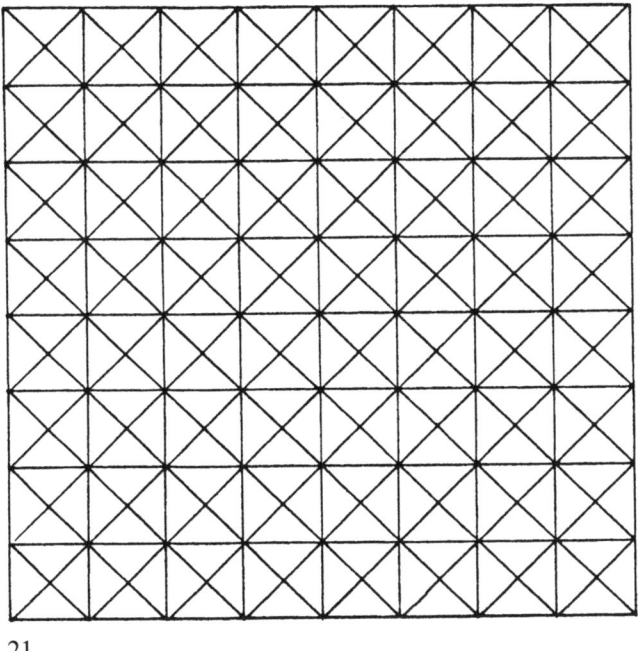
21

22

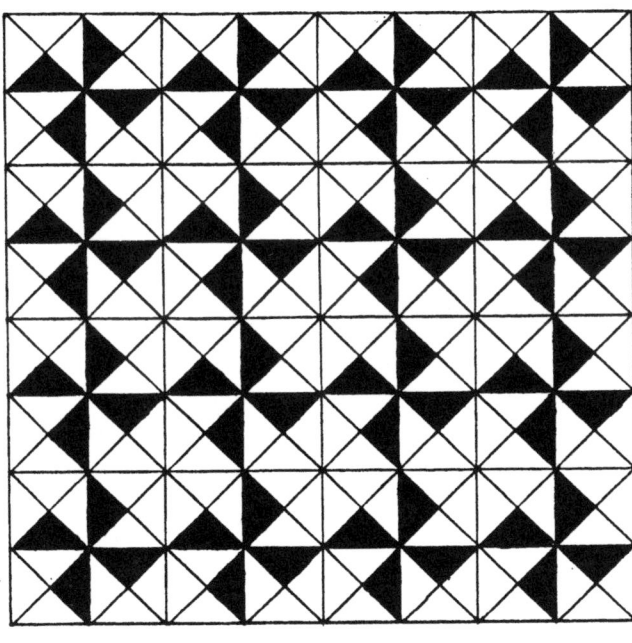
23

24

TRIANGLES AND DIAMONDS

25

26

27

28

OBTUSE TRIANGLES

29

30

31

32

SQUARES

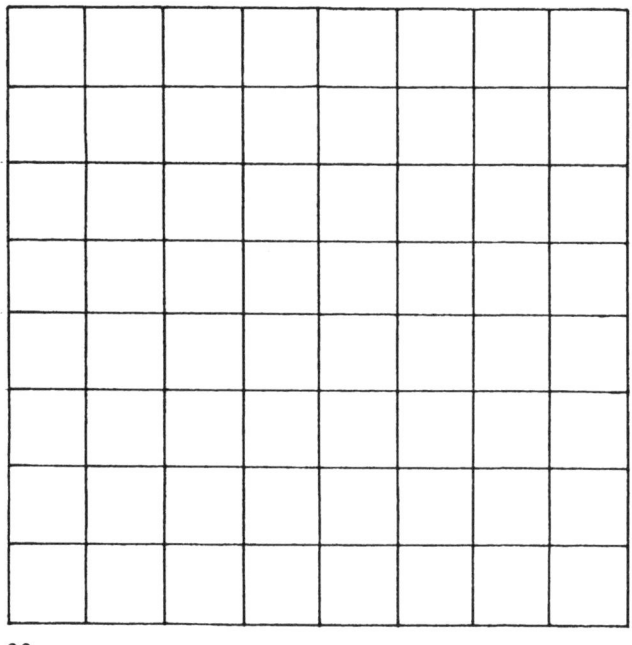
33

34

35

36

SQUARES

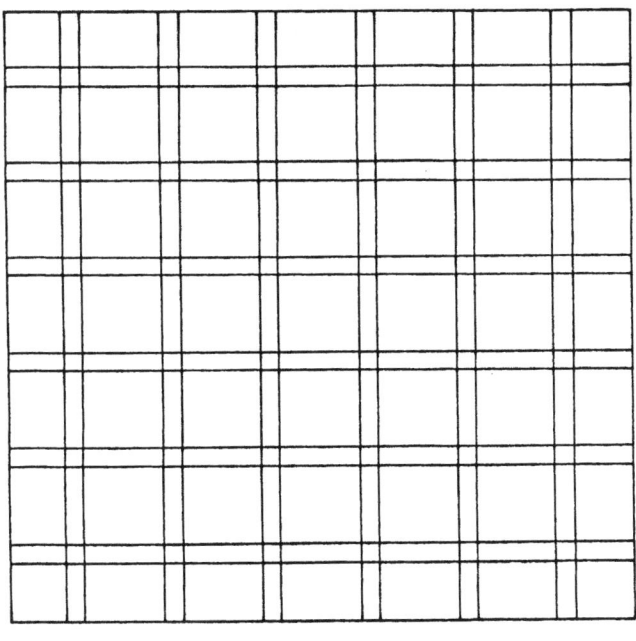
37

38

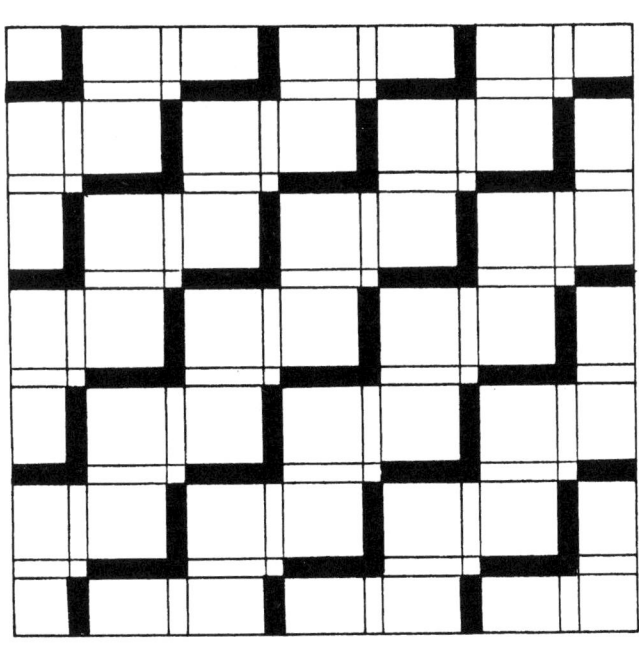
39

40

TILTED SQUARES

41

42

43

44

TILTED SQUARES

45

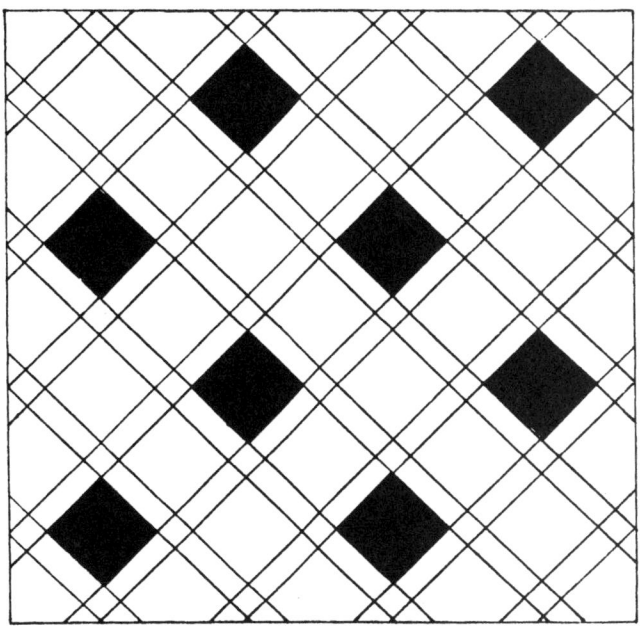

46

47

48

Alternating Rectangles

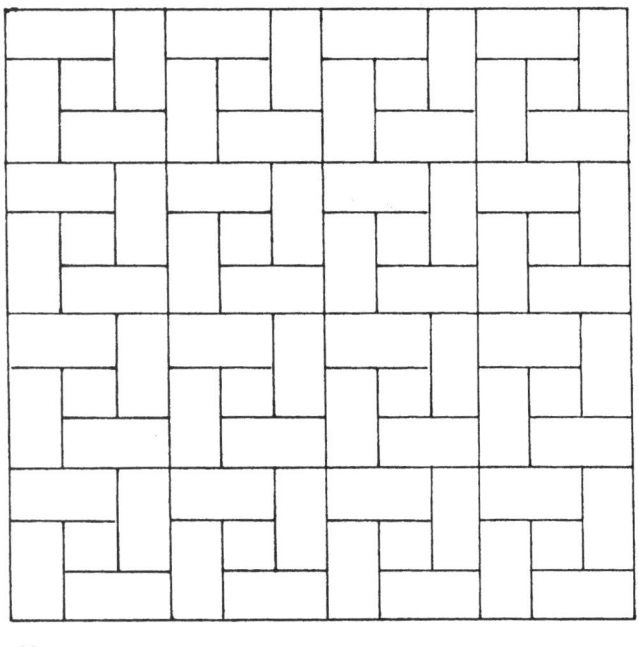

49

50

51

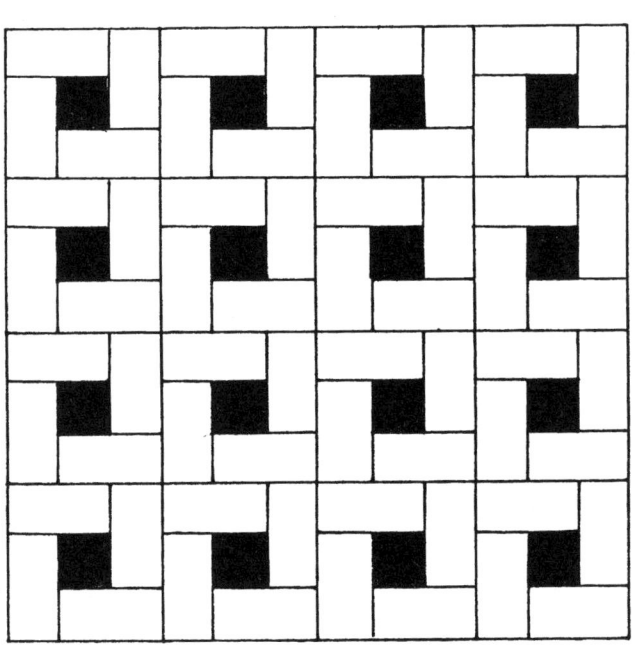

52

Horizontal Rectangles

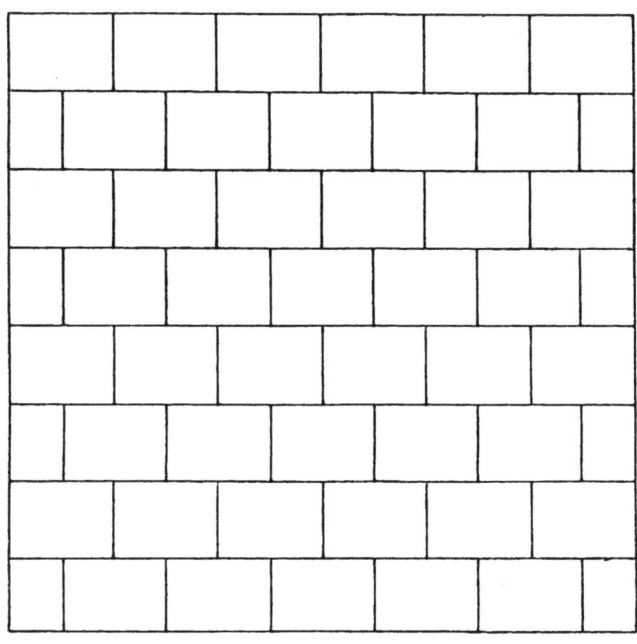
53

54

55

56

TILTED RECTANGLES

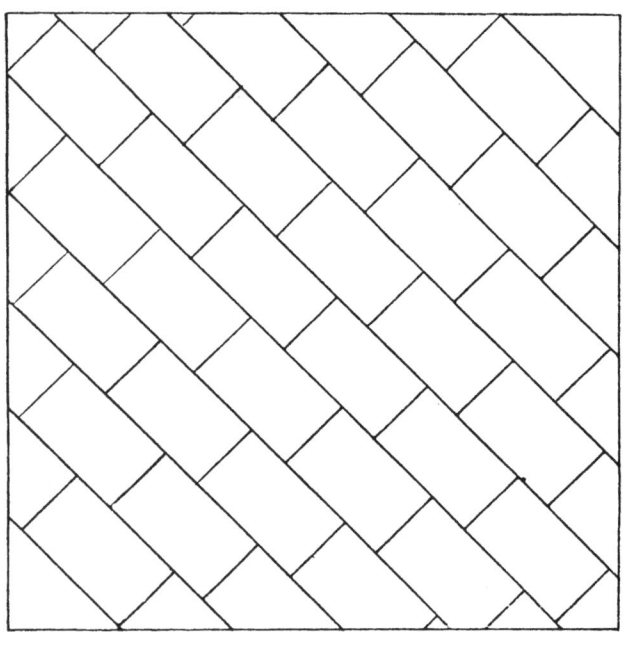
57

58

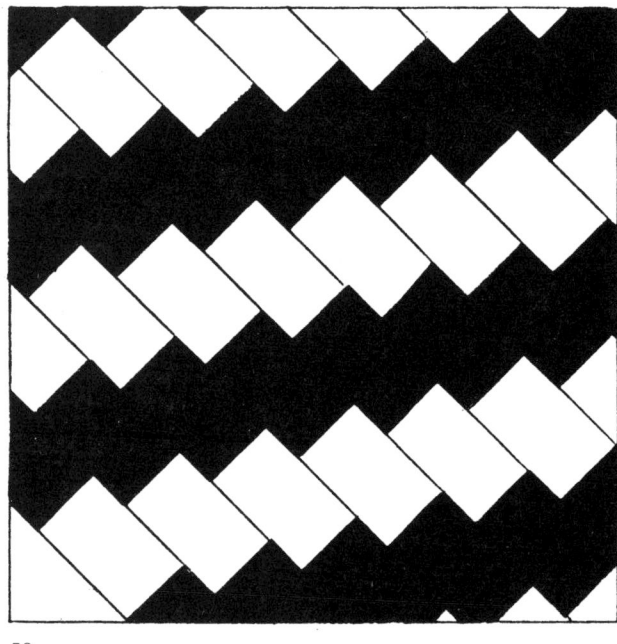
59

60

TILTED RECTANGLES

61

62

63

64

PAIRED RECTANGLES

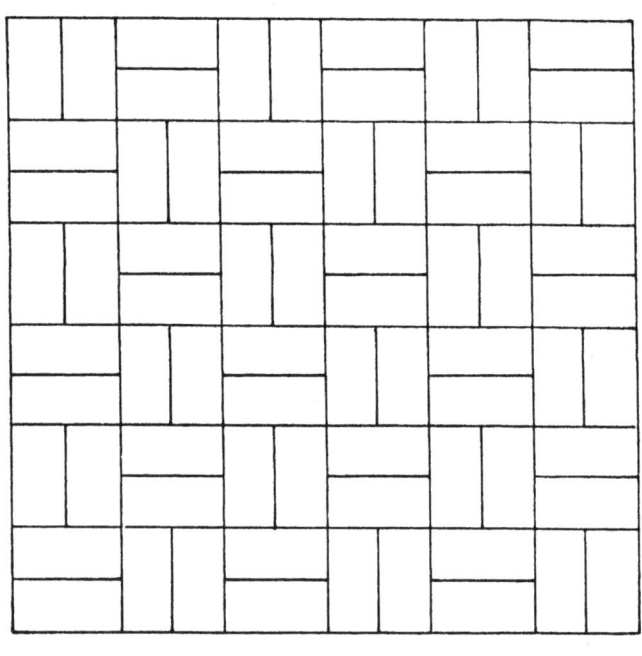

65

66

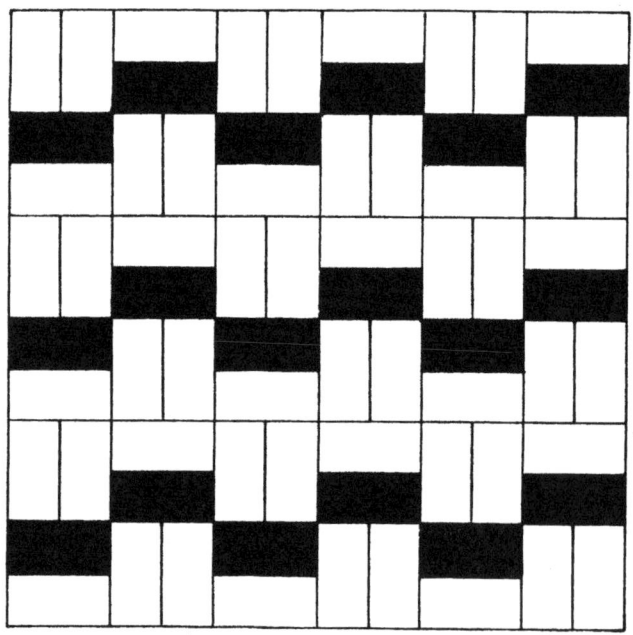

67

68

RECTANGULAR BASKETWEAVE

69

70

71

72

DIAMONDS

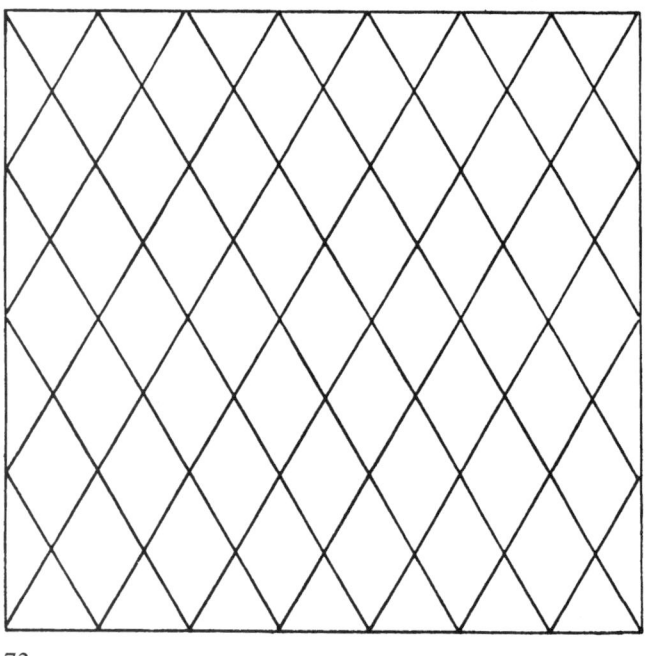

73

74

75

76

DIAMONDS

77

78

79

80

Alternating Diamonds

81

82

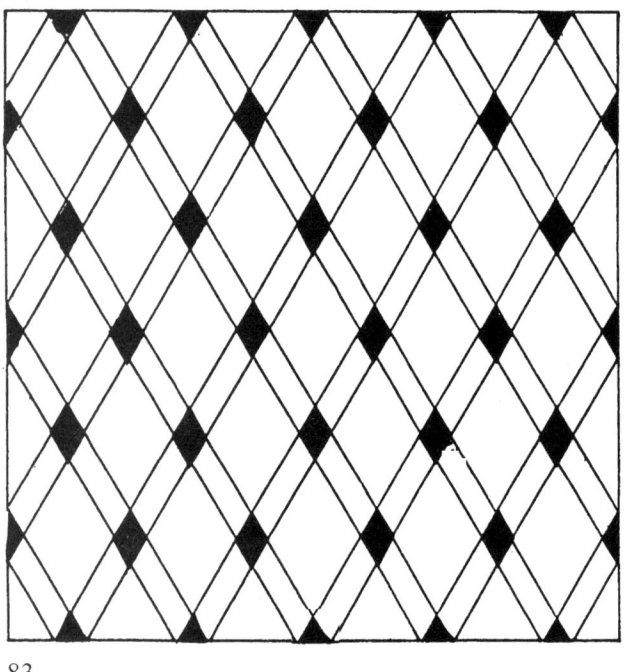
83

84

ALTERNATING DIAMONDS

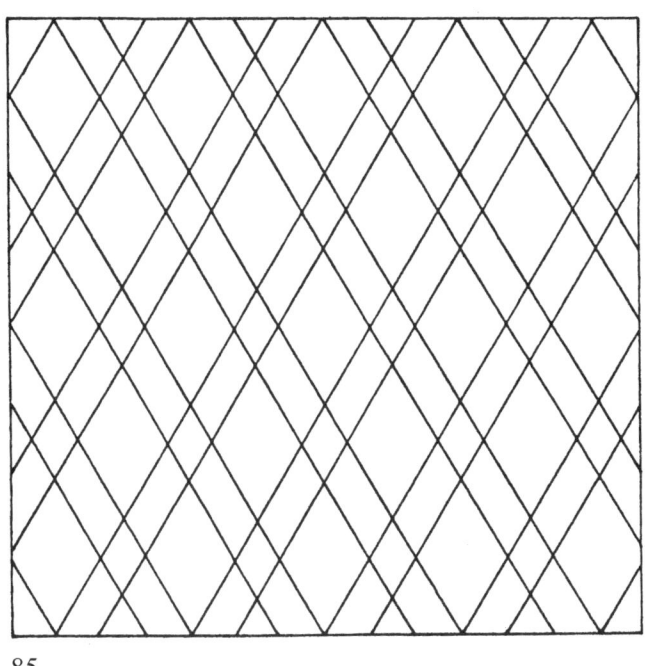
85

86

87

88

HORIZONTAL DIAMONDS

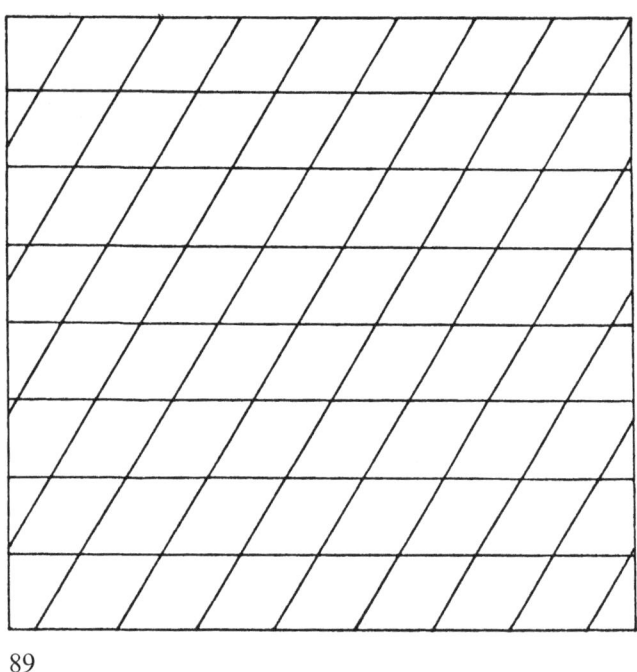
89

90

91

92

Horizontal Diamonds

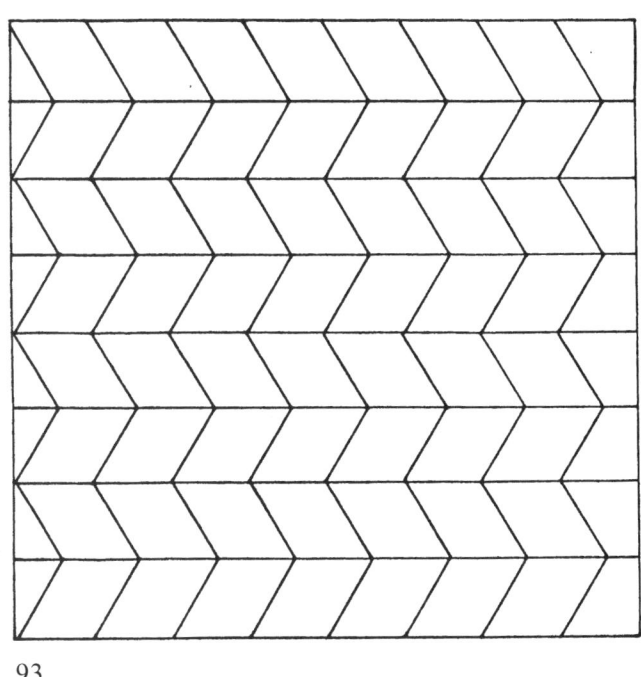
93

94

95

96

Vertical Diamonds

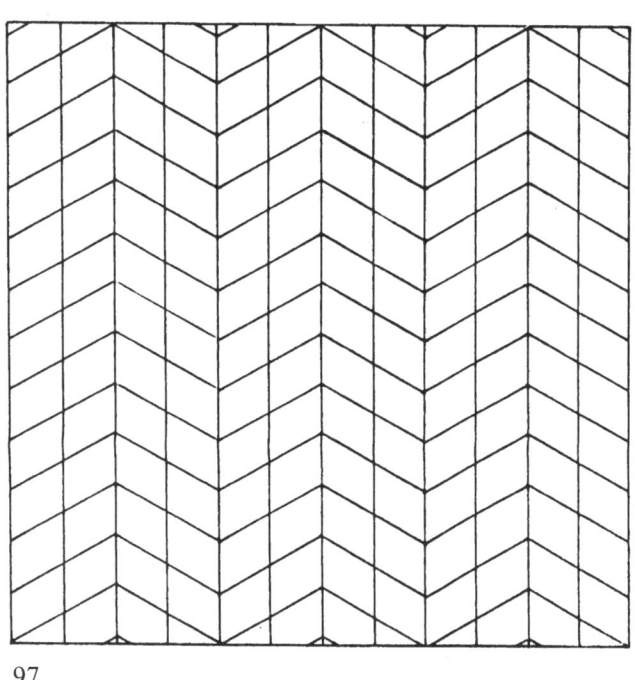
97

98

99

100

Vertical Diamonds

101

102

103

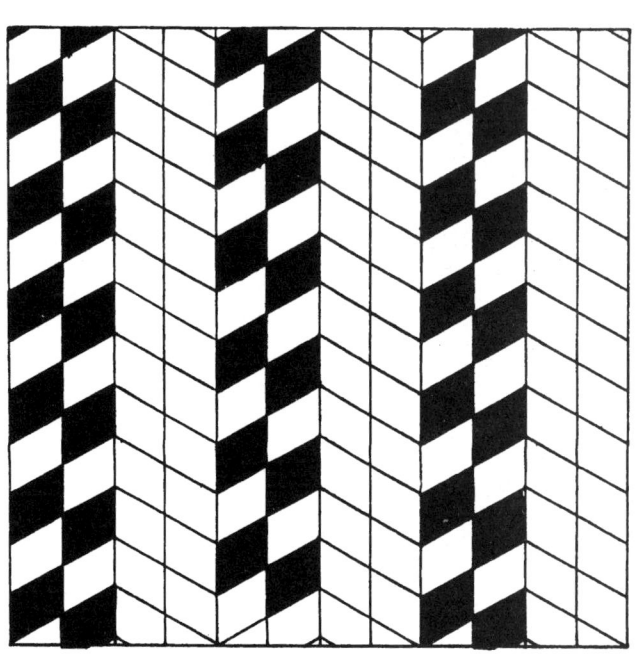
104

DIAMONDS AND CUBES

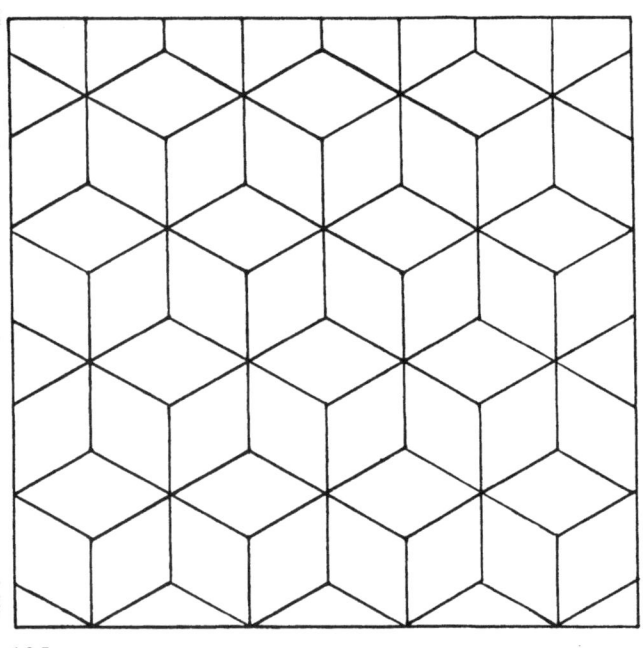
105

106

107

108

DIAMONDS AND CUBES

109

110

111

112

29

Diamonds and Cubes

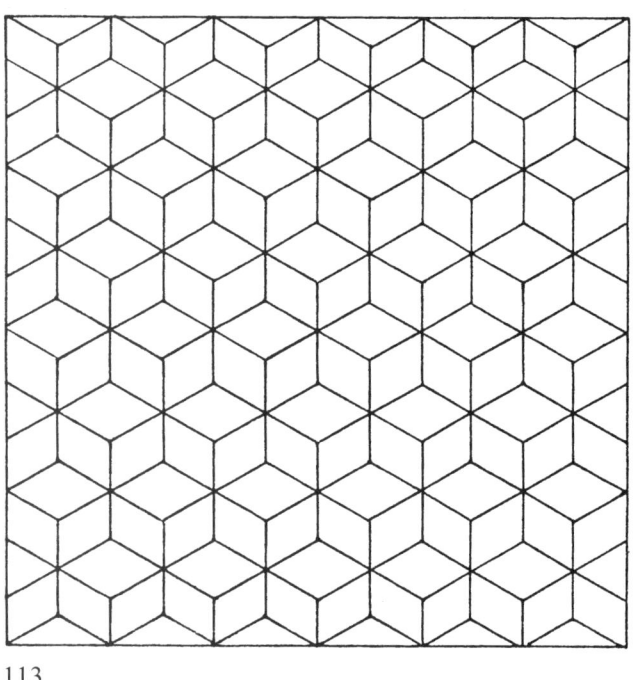
113

114

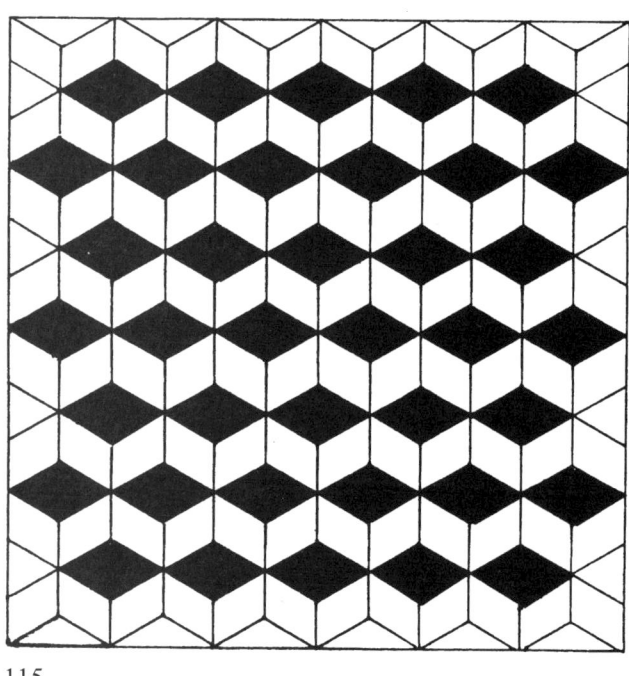
115

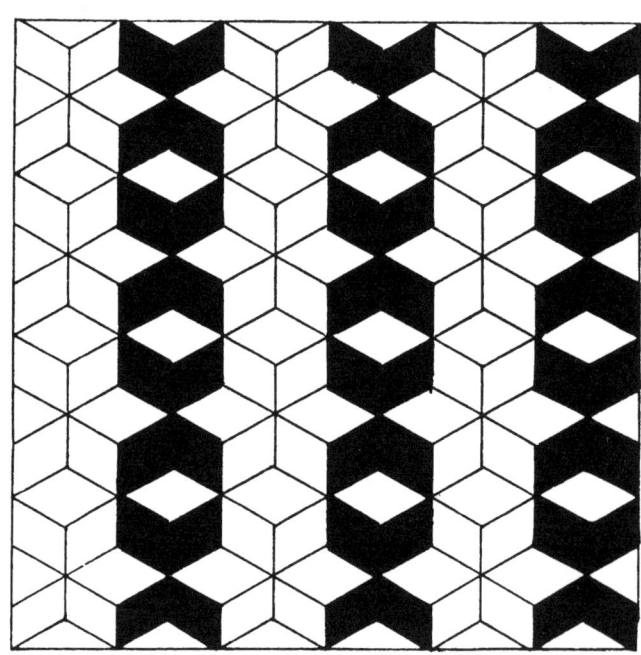
116

Diamonds and Cubes

117

118

119

120

Diamonds and Tilted Squares

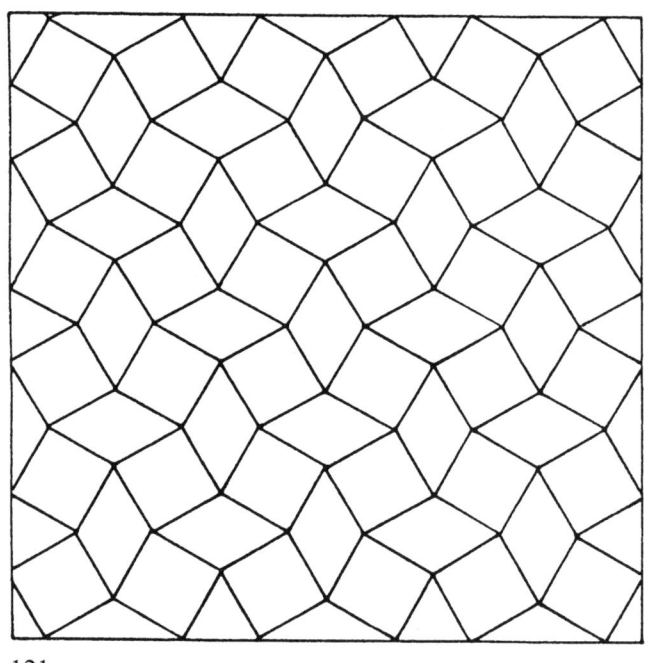
121

122

123

124

Diamonds and Tilted Squares

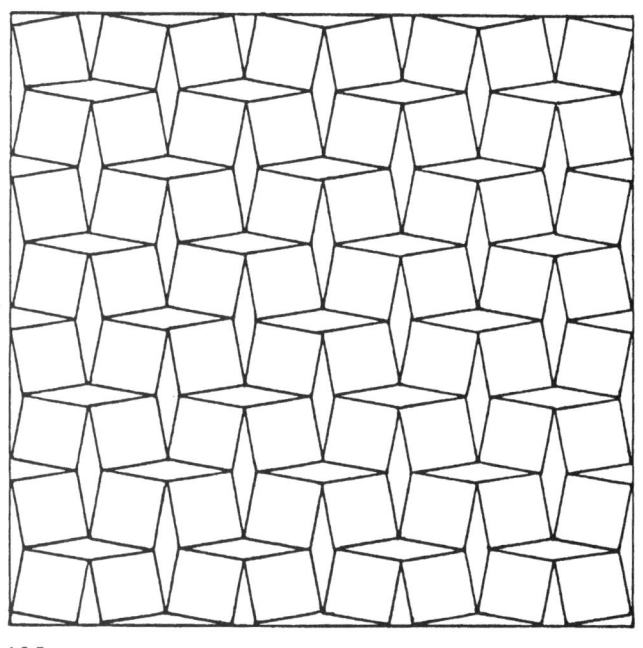
125

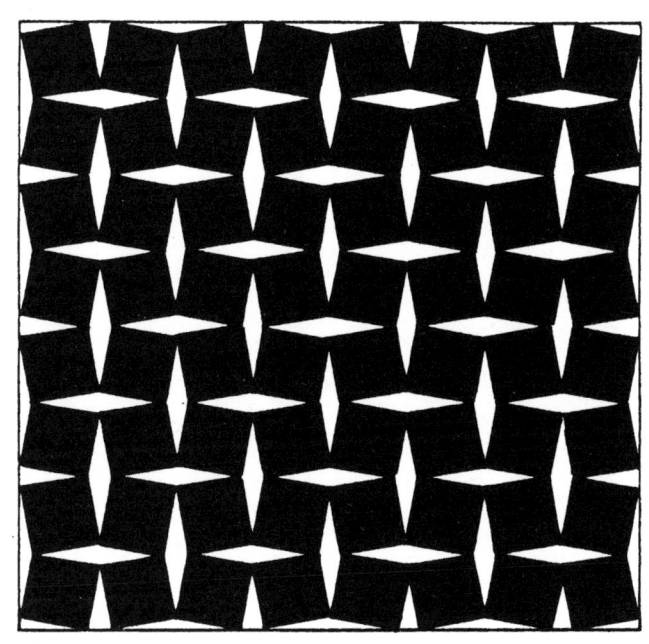
126

127

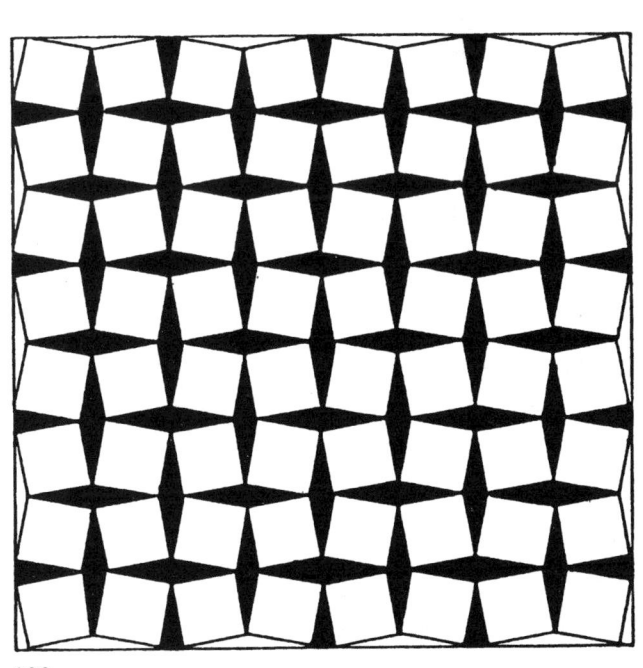
128

Diamonds and Bisected Squares

129

130

131

132

Arrangement of Diamonds

133

134

135

136

Arrangement of Hexagons

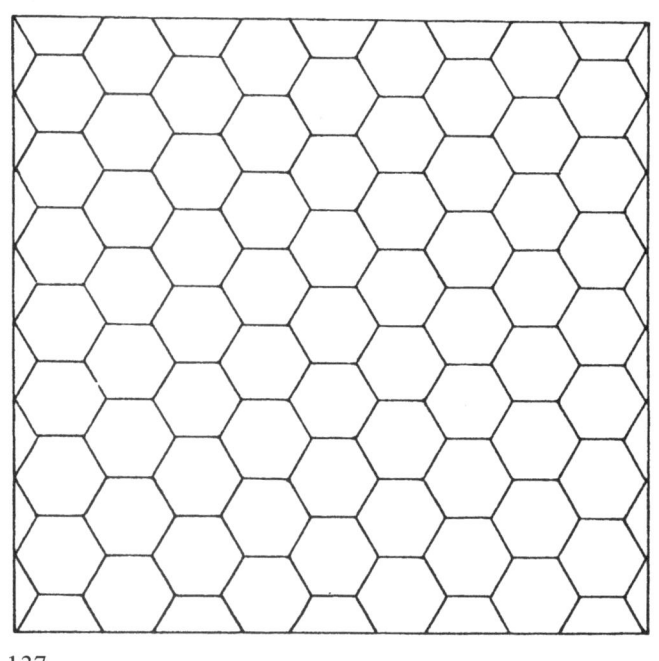
137

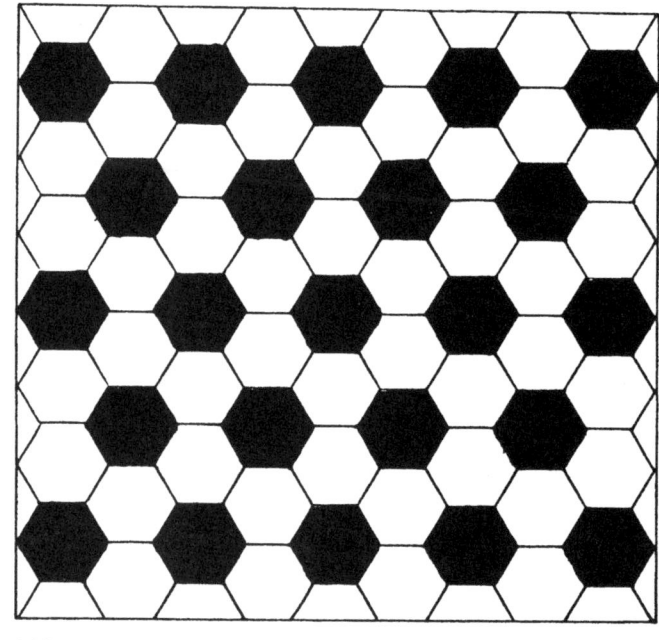
138

139

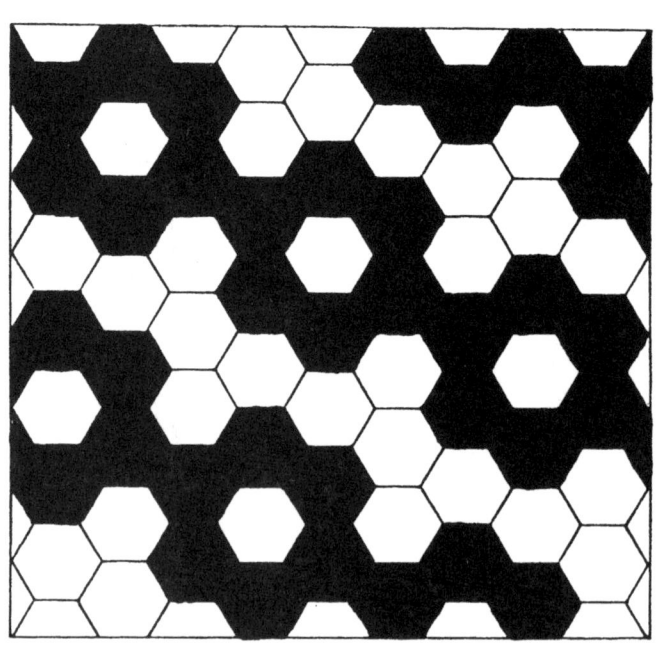
140

Arrangement of Hexagons

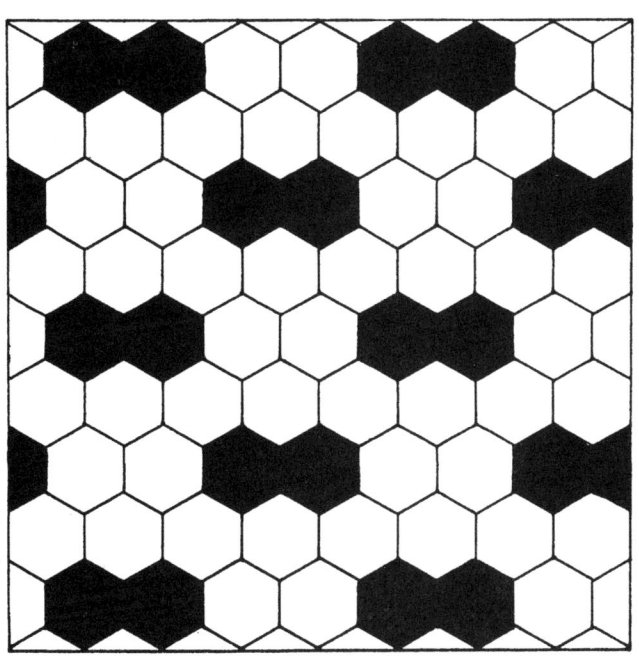

141

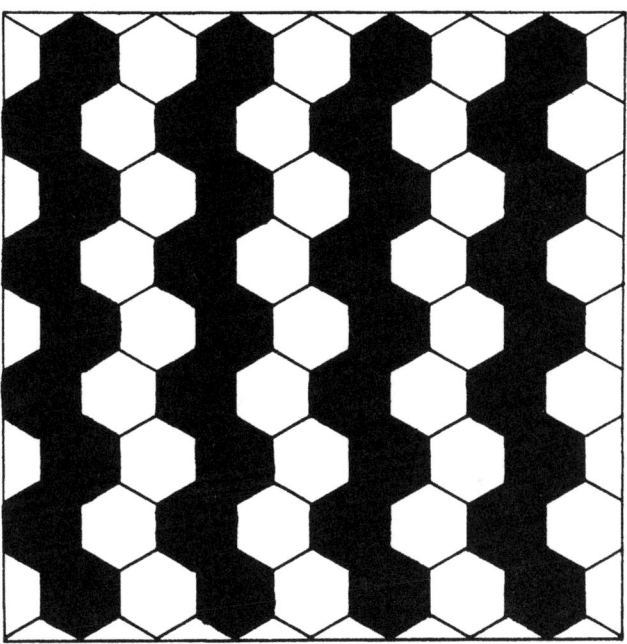

142

143

144

Arrangement of Hexagons

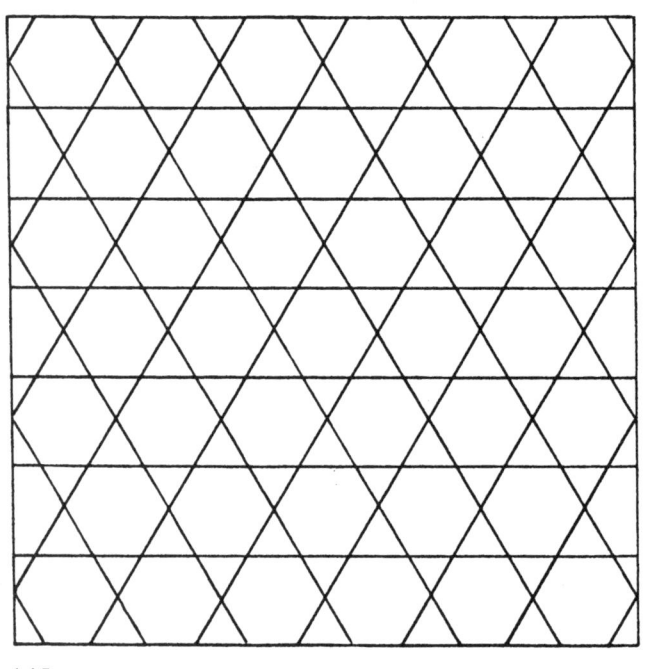

145

146

147

148

ARRANGEMENT OF HEXAGONS

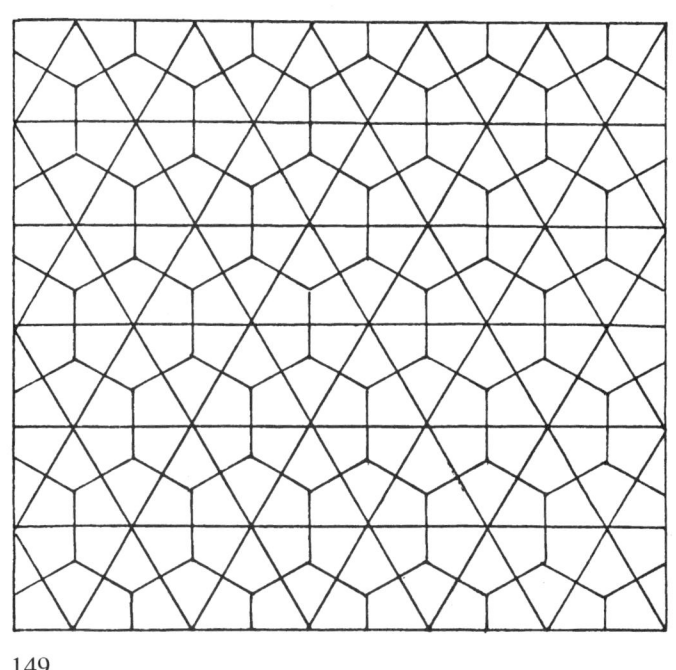

149

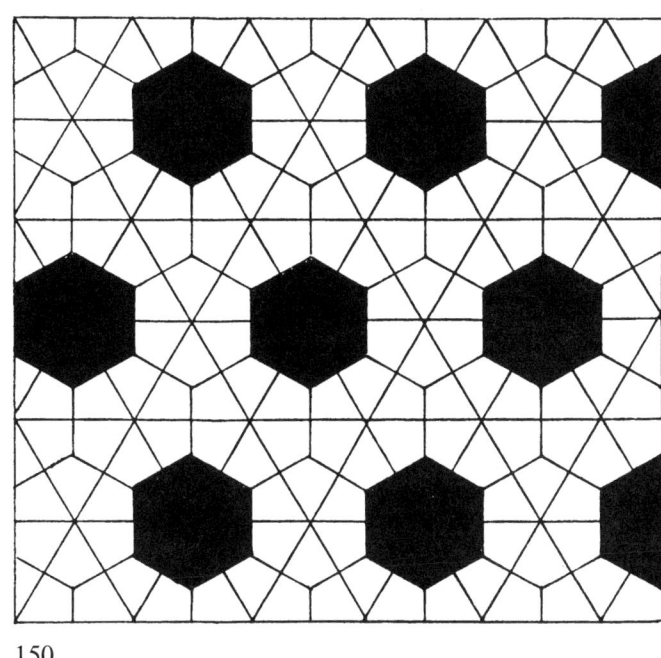

150

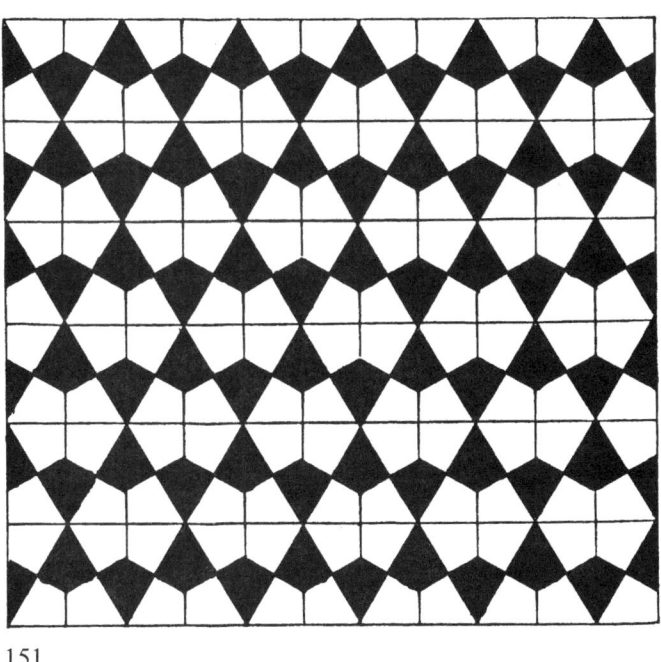

151

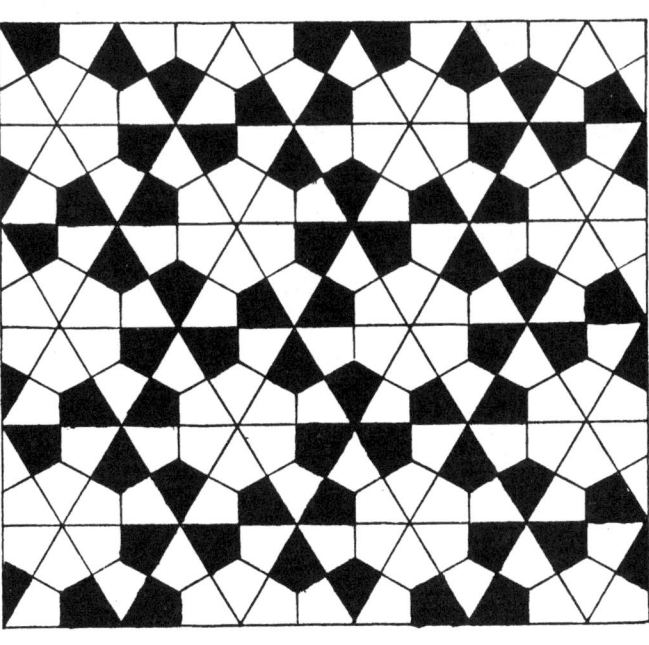

152

Arrangement of Octagons

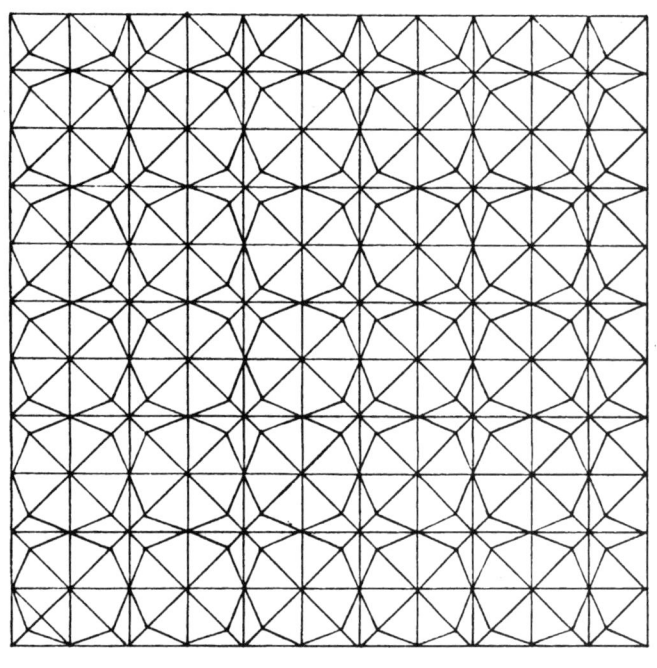

153

154

155

156

Arrangement of Octagons

157

158

159

160

Arrangement of Squares

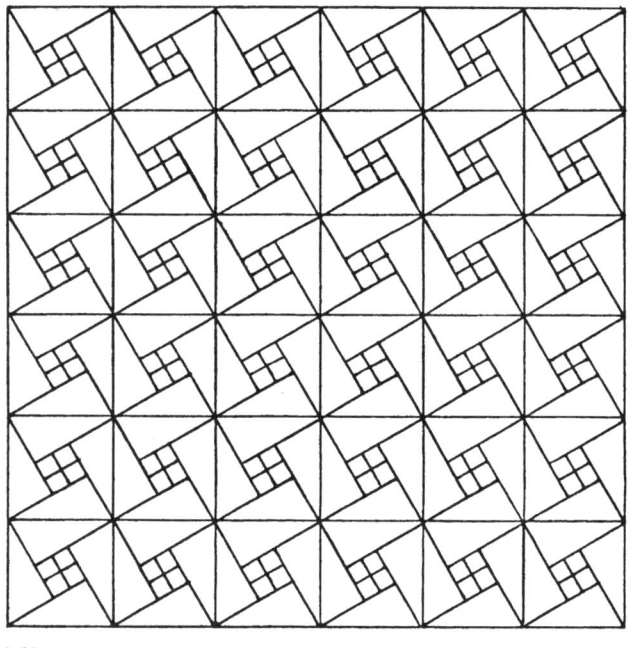

161

162

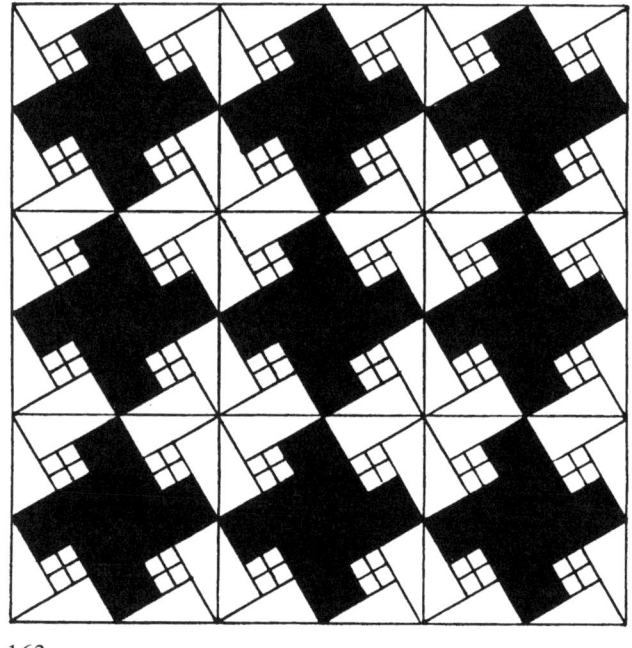

163

164